Circles and Squares

Rebecca Brooke

Name _____

Age _____

Class _____

OXFORD
UNIVERSITY PRESS

OXFORD
UNIVERSITY PRESS

Great Clarendon Street, Oxford OX2 6DP

Oxford University Press is a department of the University of Oxford.
It furthers the University's objective of excellence in research, scholarship,
and education by publishing worldwide in

Oxford New York

Auckland Cape Town Dar es Salaam Hong Kong Karachi
Kuala Lumpur Madrid Melbourne Mexico City Nairobi
New Delhi Shanghai Taipei Toronto

With offices in

Argentina Austria Brazil Chile Czech Republic France Greece
Guatemala Hungary Italy Japan South Korea Poland Portugal
Singapore Switzerland Thailand Turkey Ukraine Vietnam

OXFORD and OXFORD ENGLISH are registered trade marks of
Oxford University Press in the UK and in certain other countries

© Oxford University Press 2005

The moral rights of the author have been asserted
Database right Oxford University Press (maker)
First published 2005

2020 2019

20 19 18

No unauthorized photocopying

All rights reserved. No part of this publication may be reproduced,
stored in a retrieval system, or transmitted, in any form or by any means,
without the prior permission in writing of Oxford University Press,
or as expressly permitted by law, or under terms agreed with the appropriate
reprographics rights organization. Enquiries concerning reproduction
outside the scope of the above should be sent to the ELT Rights Department,
Oxford University Press, at the address above

You must not circulate this book in any other binding or cover
and you must impose this same condition on any acquirer

Any websites referred to in this publication are in the public domain and
their addresses are provided by Oxford University Press for information only.
Oxford University Press disclaims any responsibility for the content

ISBN 978 0 19 440094 7

Printed in China

Illustrations by: Mark Ruffle
With thanks to Sally Spray for her contribution to this series

Reading Dolphins
Notes for teachers & parents

📖 Using the book

1 Begin by looking at the first story page (page 2). Look at the picture and ask questions about it. Then read the story text under the picture with your students. **Use section 1 of the CD for this if possible.**

2 Teach and check the understanding of any new vocabulary. Note that some of the words are in the **Picture Dictionary** at the back of the book.

3 Now look at the activities on the right-hand page. Show the example to the students and instruct them to complete the activities. This may be done individually, in pairs, or as a class.

4 Do the same for the remaining pages of the book.

5 Retell the whole story more quickly, reinforcing the new vocabulary. **Sections 2 and 3 of the CD can help with this.**

6 **If possible, listen to the expanded story (section 4 of the CD). The students should follow in their books.**

7 When the book is finished, use the **Picture Dictionary** to check that students understand and remember new vocabulary. **Section 5 of the CD can help with this.**

💿 Using the CD

The CD contains five sections.

1 The story told slowly, with pauses. Use this during the first reading. It may also be used for "Listen and repeat" activities at any point.

2 The story told at normal speed. This should be used once the students have read the book for the first time.

3 The story chanted. Students may want to chant along with the story.

4 The expanded story. The story is told in a longer version. This will help the students understand English when it is spoken faster, as they will now know the story and the vocabulary.

5 Vocabulary. Each word in the **Picture Dictionary** is spoken and then used in a simple sentence.

Every Tuesday morning Mary
has art class at her school.
Mary is not happy.
She hates art.

Circle.

1 Today is (Tuesday) Thursday .

2 Mary is on at school.

3 She He is not happy.

4 Mary is a teacher student .

5 Mary likes hates art.

6 Mary is in outside the art class.

7 It is morning afternoon .

8 I like hate art class.

Mary is sitting at her desk.
She cannot draw very well.
"It's too hard," she says.

Complete the sentences.

cold   easy   big   slow
hot   hard   fast

1 $1+1=2$ It's _____ easy _____ .

2 $2{,}463 \div 473 + \sqrt{46}$ It's _____ .

3 It's _____ .

4 It's _____ .

5 It's _____ .

6 It's _____ .

7 It's _____ .

5

David is Mary's friend.
He loves art class.
He can draw very well.

What color is it? Number.

green	1	black		
orange		brown		
blue		purple		
red		yellow		

David is sitting next to Mary.
"I can help you," says David.
"Drawing is easy. I draw
shapes to help me."

Write and connect.

s<u>quare</u>

t_____

o_____

c_____

r_____

s_____

d_____

h_____

t_____

1

2

3

4

5

6

7

8

9

"Look," says David.
"You can draw a house using triangles and squares."

Circle.

1 **Mary** / (David) draws a house.

2 David draws **two** / **one** house.

3 David draws a **cat** / **house** .

4 David draws a house with **squares** / **circles** .

5 He draws it with **ovals** / **triangles** .

6 He draws it with a **heart** / **rectangle** .

7 The house has two **squares** / **triangles** .

8 David **loves** / **hates** art class.

11

"Can you draw animals with shapes?" asks Mary.
"Yes, I can," says David.

Circle yes or no .

❶ Mary wants to draw people.

yes

(no)

❷ Mary wants to draw animals.

yes

no

❸ David never draws shapes.

yes

no

❹ Mary can draw animals.

yes

no

❺ Mary is sitting at her desk.

yes

no

❻ David hates art.

yes

no

❼ Mary is showing David how to draw.

yes

no

❽ David says that drawing is easy.

yes

no

David shows Mary how to draw a dog.
"You can use circles, triangles, and ovals," he says.

Write and connect.

p<u>encil</u>

d_____

r_____

c_____

p_____

e_____

f_____

b_____

p_____

15

David shows Mary how to draw a farmer.

"You can use rectangles and diamonds," he says.

How many?

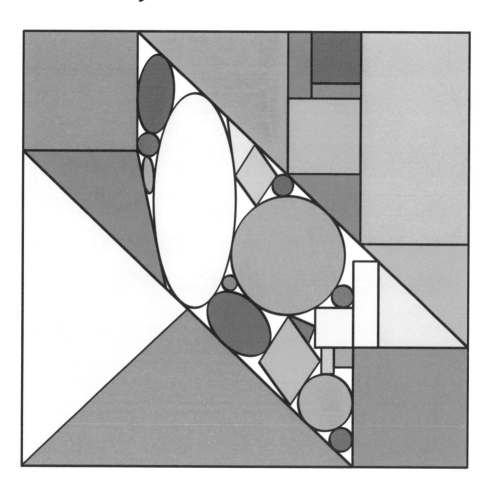

circles [7]   rectangles [ ]

ovals [ ]   diamonds [ ]

squares [ ]   triangles [ ]

"Now it's your turn. Try and draw a cat," says David. "You can use ovals and triangles."

Circle.

1 ~~(Mary)~~ David is drawing.

2 Mary is drawing a cat / dog .

3 Mary is drawing with ovals / squares .

4 Mary is drawing with a pencil / pen .

5 Mary / David is showing her how to draw.

6 Mary is happy / sad .

7 Mary's cat has a / no tail.

8 The cat's tail is a triangle / rectangle .

Now Mary can draw all on her own. She draws a picture of a beautiful farm.

How many?

sheep 3   horses ☐

dogs ☐   cats ☐

cows ☐   rabbits ☐

Mary likes art now, and she loves art class on Tuesday mornings.

Complete the sentences.

cat class loves Tuesday
house shapes farm draw

❶ Every _Tuesday_ morning Mary has art class.

❷ David loves art _____.

❸ David helps Mary to _____.

❹ David draws _____ to help him.

❺ David can draw a _____ with triangles and squares.

❻ Mary draws a _____.

❼ Then Mary draws a _____.

❽ Now Mary _____ art class.

Picture Dictionary

black

desk

blue

diamond

brown

green

circle

heart

cow

horse

orange

rectangle

oval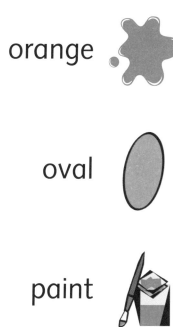

red

paint

sheep

purple

square

rabbit

triangle

Dolphin Readers

Dolphin Readers are available at five levels, from Starter to 4.

The Dolphins series covers four major themes:

Grammar, Living Together, The World Around Us, Science and Nature.

For each theme, there are two titles at every level.

Activity Books are available for all Dolphins.

All Dolphins are available on audio CD.

(2 TITLES ON EACH CD 💿 SEE TABLE BELOW)

Teacher's Notes are available at **www.oup.com/elt/dolphins**

	Grammar	Living Together	The World Around Us	Science and Nature
Starter	• Silly Squirrel • Monkeying Around	• My Family • A Day with Baby	• Doctor, Doctor • Moving House	• A Game of Shapes • Baby Animals
Level 1	• Meet Molly • Where Is It?	• Little Helpers • Jack the Hero	• On Safari • Lost Kitten	• Number Magic • How's the Weather?
Level 2	• Double Trouble • Super Sam	• Candy for Breakfast • Lost!	• A Visit to the City • Matt's Mistake	• Numbers, Numbers Everywhere • Circles and Squares
Level 3	• Students in Space • What Did You Do Yesterday?	• New Girl in School • Uncle Jerry's Great Idea	• Just Like Mine • Wonderful Wild Animals	• Things That Fly • Let's Go to the Rainforest
Level 4	• The Tough Task • Yesterday, Today and Tomorrow	• We Won the Cup • Up and Down	• Where People Live • City Girl, Country Boy	• In the Ocean • Go, Gorillas, Go